THE BODY CAN
TOLERATE

ALSO BY LORIA MENDOZA

Life's Too Short

THE BODY CAN
TOLERATE

POEMS

LORIA MENDOZA

RED LIGHT LIT

The Body Can Tolerate
Loria Mendoza

Copyright © 2025 by Loria Mendoza
All rights reserved.

No part of this book may be reproduced, stored in a retrieval system, or transmitted in any form or by any means—electronic, mechanical, photocopying, recording, or otherwise—without the prior written permission of both the publisher and the copyright owner, except in the case of brief quotations used in critical articles or reviews. For information contact Red Light Lit.

Published by Red Light Lit Press
557 8th Avenue, San Francisco, CA 94118
redlightlit.com

Library of Congress Control Number:
2025942819
ISBN: 978-0-9998895-3-4

Cover Art: Leah Bury
Book Design and Layout: Leah Bury, Jennifer Lewis, and Loria Mendoza
Edited by Isra Cheema

This is a work of original poetry. Any resemblance to real persons, living or dead, is purely coincidental or used with permission.

For all of my ghosts, living and dead.

And for Andromeda.

CONTENTS

I. Ghosts of Family   1
First You Must Enter   2
Memory of Light   4
Some Things Are the Same Thing   5
Prophetic Dreams   6
Parakeets and Swallows   8
Invasive Species   10
When I Leave You, Mother, I Don't
   Bother Saying Goodbye   11
Sisters   13
Thoughts Preceding the Attack   15
Thank You For the Skin   18
Not Anymore, Not Like This   19

II. Ghosts of Love   31
Bricks   32
Hook and Light   33
I Think I Might Be the Toxic Person
   You Need To Cut Out of Your Life   35
Beautiful, Beautiful   37
Spit   38
Trapped   40
Angel   42
Lamb   44
Are You Okay?   46
Deforming   47
Philadelphia   48
Second Thoughts   49
Despite the Danger   50
How Is Our Love Related To Your
   Trauma, He Asks   52
Flat   54
Hold Me, Damn It   56
Etymology   57
Cheers   58
Backdraft   59
To Love Is To Change Everything   61

III. Ghosts of Self   63
Defining Loss   64
Cardinal   66
Geometry of Hunger   70
It Turns Out That No One Thinks
   I'm a Bird   72
I Research Mad Women   73
Gossip   74
Youth   75
Embers   77
Cracked Mirror   78
Penumbra   79
Emptiness   83
What Stayed In My Skin   84
Awakening   86
Coda For Andromeda   88

Notes   93

THE BODY CAN
TOLERATE

GHOSTS OF FAMILY[1]

---

[1] Sit with the feeling of the body
a map etched in blood, atom, bone
occupied by losses I would not bear
yet feel. I want to name them
instead, whisper, *wasp nest*
sorrow, scribble dreams left hanging, cut
telephone wires sparking
heat in the silence.

This body, a vault of heirlooms
ticking clocks in abandoned rooms
dust gathering in empty jars
there is little time—
less sweetness left
after all that has soured in wait

reliving, relieving.
This body, my inheritance
woven of unspoken histories
braided from bloodlines
slick with memory

this story begins. When I was
unraveled from my mother
I did not cry but spoke—
the sound made her laugh
then weep.
I reached for her
am reaching, still—
what I would give to hear
her voice without grief.

This is how I began:
yearning pressed into
the marrow, electric, my mouth
determined to ask
who does this medicine—
this body—belong to?

FIRST YOU MUST ENTER

There's a door in my hair I've only just discovered
where my dreams have grown opposable thumbs.

I sleep little to keep their swelling hands still,
retell stories
to put their sins to bed
my fingernails filed into lock picks,
my windmill arms swinging out at exits—

the moment my grandmother's gold is clawed
from my finger
thrown into the night, colossal as birth
my own dextrous patterns, undoing me.

I never see the ring again,
    I go on searching, hands stretched out
    like a newborn thing.

My left arm disappears for no reason
reappears under my pillow when I make the bed.
I scream every time before I realize it's mine,
hear grandmother's voice pucker like apple mouth:

this thing you inhabit is embodied
how can you not believe in ghosts?
don't you believe   in your own body
what it houses when you dream?   what kept you?
what do you think all your anxiety is about
if not the pull between possession
and exorcism?

I pass a calving on the freeway
the closeness of life
caressing the fragrance of birth into
my open mouth

beams of light illuminate the breeder's
bloody hands
ripping consciousness from one body
into the next unknown
madness of night—
life doesn't just begin   it negates.

My hair full of night sweat whips in the wind
ghosts soar howling out the window like flies.

MEMORY OF LIGHT

I rub my eyes, back to the door, an invisible current between me and the exit. In the yard, a child lets out a restless shriek, a declaration of joy that you sleep through. I do not need to turn around—I have lived here long enough to know your neighbors, but not long enough to be known by them the way I know each day I'm alive breaks open, water struck by a body before it sinks. I tilt back a yawn, hold my breath, calculate the seconds that separate joy from terror—the time it takes to sink in between each moment: my mouth open tasting rain for the first time, my father's return from California, his coffee stained teeth breathing a warning into my skin, synthetic yarn across my tear stained cheeks when grandmother died and left us crocheted blankets. My mother's apology when she thought the cancer had gotten down to the last bite of her. My divorce. The lover that followed who opened new seams. The taste of blood. Drunk and on pills, he smashed my nose into my skull. The taste of his mouth as I returned. The feeling of peeling myself away from him like meat from the bone. When I smoke a cigarette I always cross my legs the same way—balance the filter in the same corner of my mouth—wonder if it's the repetition that's killing me or perhaps the pattern is loving you, the thrill in being here, knowing I'm not supposed to be.

SOME THINGS ARE THE SAME THING

Which ghost fastens my necklace in the morning
hands like my mother's, fingers like mine
markings on the skin that give it away.

What words the dead scribble upon my mirror
are the jewels pointed up or down into my skin
am I bleeding or just seeing spots
am I Lady Macbeth or corpse posing
what sign will I fail to notice
where did I put those teeth

what purpose, this recurring dream
the closed-off well in the yard
the elephant canna lily   receding to see-through
decay hatching underfoot

loud as cicadas.

We find small toys and sandals in the pale foliage
wonder if it ate up the children we once were
if it still eats   if we are still
children
too afraid to look down the well
finding something terrible
a splinter that won't surface
picked to the tilt of septicity.

We become walking wounds
unable to find the spot
where pain is buried
we just keep picking and digging at sores
that aren't where we left them
we burrow like animals, sensing only hunger
        to unbury what won't die.

PROPHETIC DREAMS

I inherited my father's talkative dreams, made difficult by our repetitive loss of teeth. I dream I see him at arm's length, waiting from the periphery to understand what I'm trying to say. I mouth every word, consider the weight of each choice, yet when I speak, they come out as soft mumbles of alarm. Still, he tries so hard to hear me that he forgets his own rotting teeth rooting him to his body, to his life. He parts his lips, and his tongue floats out from his mouth. He pulls himself up the length of it, a rope to the sky.

My father told me that life is too short, life is too unfair. For brief moments of time, these truths are more than my determined heart can take. The older I get the more teeth I lose, and the more I understand that conversation does not come from the outside. That the truth can be spoken, yet remain unheard.

The older my father gets, the more fiercely he listens, albeit in dreams. The less he understands, the more he relies on my promise to remember what he's already told me. To turn over what I've learned until something true spills out. We don't speak at the dinner table—he's not much of a talker, or perhaps he's afraid that no one's listening. Still, I've forgotten how to stay still long enough not to panic about my own rate of decay while pushing peas around with my fork.

I finger my molars upon waking to feel if they're secure. Sometimes I think they feel loose. I ask my lover to wiggle one for me just to be sure. Sometimes they are firmly rooted in my head and anyone that ever loved me is dead. I reach out.

My lover has disappeared. There is nothing but an empty room and my rotting teeth buried deep in my skull.

I don't tell my father how I think I'm losing my mind. In dreams disguised as memory, we lose each other again and again, in partings yet to come. I look at his smile, full of gaps and sincerity, and wonder when we bury him, who will water the garden and know what is a flower and what is a weed—if I can unroot one without the other. *It's all one system*, I heard him say once. I think of my body, of my bones and veins rooting me in place as I reach out my hands, trying to cup every hurt I've ever witnessed falling from him.

Every spring I watch him in the garden, shaking the dirt from the uproots of a weed like a tiny head he holds by the hair, clumps of dirt and rock falling away like my teeth, like my dreams upon waking. I watch as he sends mound after mound of crabgrass sailing through the air, waiting for the *ping* as they land in the wheelbarrow he carts back and forth across the yard. I want to ask about the violence of not being loved. Of not knowing, really knowing, the people who love us. But the second I open my mouth to speak, my father's teeth fall out of my head into the wheelbarrow before me. I cart them across the yard and wonder, *what ever happened to my daughter?*

PARAKEETS AND SWALLOWS

Anxiety came this way:
with every slap
a parakeet starved in her cage.
I prayed the love I carried would fade
and it did.

My mother blamed me for the rape
and the birds as well.
Now the seeds feed the ants.
I wince at the raising
of a wing or a hand.

The repeating of history seems almost scientific—
ever expanding   before collapsing upon itself.

Who else could my mother blame?
What happened
made her.

My grandmother long dead from the overdose,
yet untame from the memory
of turning her head, walking away.

Every crime is always the mother's
even when she's just a girl.

My mother's jaw never unclenched to speak of it
after spilling her venom into my small body.
A bitter potion, and like Alice I grew
in knowledge, not wonder.

I was eleven when she told me
to go unraped,
my throat, a feathered thing fallen from the hand,
gasping skyward
a *horrible lucky girl*.

We gave different names to our inheritance as our
jaws grinded away
our tongues raw from chewing what silence left.

I kept grandmother's teeth when she died,
pried each tooth loose from the cotton-
candy-colored acrylic gums,
shaped them into little apologies and held them up
to my mother.

Sometimes years go by and we don't speak—
that's how tired we are,
how much we've failed at love.

Still, I drink the coffee,
wait for hunger each morning,
rebel against starvation
despite the pills and the powders,
venomous drink and love
survive despite being emptied like my mother's
purse
some receipt or faded memory
tumbling onto the worn spot on the couch.

Mother, I want to give you sweetness
despite your hand on my bird-like throat
coaxing a bitter swallow.
My teeth gnashing.

INVASIVE SPECIES

Looking behind the shower curtain
afraid of monsters and bad men, I realize
it's fear and love
I can't stand—

how they raised me
shared the belt
found every hiding place
how they knew everything   or pretended to
the way God does.

But when we were young I knew the child in the
mirror
better than anyone

she's older now   brought to terror by
a gentle wind.

Oh, how I loved her
unmindful of her heart's spillage—
how beautiful.

Heads round as globe thistle, we laughed, her head
erupting
a million blue flowers.

Now she's gone to seed
a grenade of thorns eager to pierce through skin.

I keep my head down
watch where I step.

WHEN I LEAVE YOU, MOTHER, I DON'T BOTHER SAYING GOODBYE

We hurl watermelon
slice after slice like knives

trade turns strapped to the target
swirling red and white wheel
perched on backyard cinder blocks.

We miss on purpose—a kindness
and a fear of what it means to win the war.

When sweet melon is pulp
smashed, dripping pink
we heave whatever we can dig up
impossible grief disguised as potatoes
dog bones
bulbs just blossoming
arms sculpted from unburying
until one day there is nothing kind
left
between us,
only some dead thing
dug up,
dragged in
a trail of blood you deny like a child gone quiet
with guilt.
I tell you, *I'm not playing this game anymore.*

The remains of love move inside
follow us room to room.
Flies creep in—
our wounds draining into their mouths.
You refuse to believe
me
like you refuse anesthesia
vaccines and therapy
overdosing on aspirin nose bleeds

spitting watermelon seeds
at an empty wheel

your red country teeth baptized
in the hate you choke up and swallow

souring what's left of you.

SISTERS

We blossomed
    through cunning pavement,
        little knives between our lips

cutting through
    shame,
        sirens,

the ingrown years spent
    beating our fists
        against whatever we could find to hit—

whatever dared to think itself
    out of reach
        or silent—

how dare the quiet shush us—

we wondered
    and waited
        for the world to resound

but it never did

no matter how loud
    we yelled, we had nothing
        to prove but the tortuousness of
            battlefields—

learned our powerlessness early
    from every *just ignore them*
        that carved us
            into *them*

scooping crooked bangs
    from our eyes—
        we stared into a fridge filled with food
            that smelled green.

Come summer we dewormed honeydew,
    opened and closed the freezer door
        practicing what we thought was magic

but we never made anything
    appear that we could eat—
        just desire
            rising in our throats.

We can't remember how
    but somehow we knew
        exactly what we were missing

from the way other people
    locked their doors
        when we walked by,

dreaming of Capri-Suns in our throats
    and neon Band-Aids
        on our duct-taped knees.

We walked with bare feet
    colored with summer gravel,
        our sweaty faces like two rabbits
            pulled from a hat.

Whistling through blades of grass—
    we mastered the mastery of a trick
        not to make something appear—

but to keep on vanishing.

THOUGHTS PRECEDING THE ATTACK

It's thunderstorm country
and the last candle has gone out
I guess it was just done burning.

I've gone out
I've gone gone. I've talked to myself,
waiting for the void to answer.

Sometimes the devil you summon
in the dark
is yourself.

I rely on memory
hammer forgetful toes into wooden legs
scraps of life

is this land still
free? We learn
to memorize our relation to it in the dark—

even with broken-window-daylight ticking through
the cracks, we can't walk in our home
without breaking—

shadowed in what we can't afford
and can't afford to lose.
Questions rise from the virus

popping like corn in our throats
while enemies
surround us like asbestos—

What kind of cancer?
Generational poverty?
We weren't meant to survive the sickness,

my father shook his head at the mutation
I guess that's where I get it from—
bleeding handful of nails and no hammer

the dreams of his father's country cut off midstory
because he no longer remembered the language.
I began to catalog what seized under the tyranny:

his back
his breath
his knees

his skin
once so richly cradled in reds and browns
one knew how lovingly the earth had birthed him.

He told me and I listened
because it was all I could do for him.
That's fortune, a coming and going

the way a candle always goes out when it's done
burning and it's a dark vigil
after Thoughts and Prayers

are offered the only light in the room.
By this time we know existence goes both ways
nostalgia in the middle of nowhere

the way my mother is a system
the way my memory is an operator
What is it to you, anyway?

she loves to ask me
as if I'm not shining with what she's reflected
upon me. It's everything to me—

she is my country and all I've ever known is exile
and ruin after a storm.
I sleep where I can

wonder if I'll I see her again
she who held me like a blade
taught me to fear falling on what she'd made sharp

the terror of snakes that swim into childless
wombs, how to undo myself as quickly as my
shoes, to fear obscurity in the rituals of poverty

as much as death, and I
belonging to no one but the observer
have never been so afraid.

As a child we always say,
carrying the corpse of what's rotted inside—
where was I? Oh, yes—

As a child, the dog lived and slept outside
behind the click of a shackle beyond a door
disquiet reaching like a disease—

there were no flags left to surrender.
I waved a white seashell in the yard
so small.

THANK YOU FOR THE SKIN

Thank you for the skin
I carry
and shudder
dart beneath and powder
each touch a generous ache
bound to my halted face
under this fascist simulacrum
whitewashed, pistol-whipped,
iced and incarcerated
the skin I ask you to love
is criminal
I know
cannot unknow
I press my lips to each hollow
hide it from harm when it bulges ripe
pinch it when it starts to cry
break its fingers one by one
until they all point toward joy.

NOT ANYMORE, NOT LIKE THIS

1.
Elbows bent
    into the shape
of an eye,
      I suck on brown limes
          until only pith remains
    then dunk them
          into empty
              shot glasses.
The walls smell of bleach
            and rot,
  a little like Red 40
maraschino cherry sewage,
          and something in here
    smells like
        her—
    but
        she's dead,
so I should say
        something in here smells like
          she *used* to smell
            before
              she died.

2.
Someone
has rubbed off my lipstick
      with the back of
         my hand.
    It's
      the color
        of my parents'
       garage
      that has never
    been painted,
not even after

    the man who was
       as old then
              as I am now
     hung himself
          from a rafter
  one floor below
       where I slept.

You can't
             paint over
                        death,
my mother said,

     you can't
            erase
                    a thing
    that has
              ( )
                            happened.

3.
I think about
    the first time I
    saw a ghost,
    or at least
    part of one
    because there was only
    the spotted arm
    erasing itself,
    its twisted skin
    kissed
    with
                sun bruises
    left in my bed
    like
    the tooth fairy
    had brought it.

But the tooth fairy
    is only
              family.
I know this now,
how a family pays
for each other's
trauma
in one way
or another,
how some call this
just what families do,
how others call this
         hell.

4.
That's what I tell
        the man
who has sat down
      right next to me
  when there are
  twenty other
        empty
          seats
        in the room.
How my mother is a ghost sometimes.
                But she's not
    dead,
        just
        dissipating
  like   breath
        on a car window,
burying herself in the past,
   still taking the trouble
to say
      things I can't quite
        make out
or would want to

even
        if
                I could.

But
        the general consensus is
                love
                + time
                = labor.

The woman gave birth to you,
the man says, as if I don't already know.
Yet it is for that
                        fact alone,
I
    unbury her
                        with one of the broken
shovels
she keeps
        in the garage.

        It takes twice the effort

    to resurrect
                    someone
who wants
            to stay
                        buried.
(shovel
        broken—
                handle splintered)
I
  keep
        digging.

5.
My father
    helped me find it.
He knows
        where
            the broken
things go   so he can   fail
                to remember
other things.
He tells me
    I should talk
to my mother
        while I
            unbury her,
that the least
we can do
            for the dying
is to
   talk   and listen,
              if they
can
    be heard.
          They almost always
          can be,
but the toll
   it takes
      is akin
to narcolepsy,
and I feel
     as if I am
            sleepwalking
through life,
   marching
               straight
toward
my own
        death.

6.
I don't know, what do you think?
I ask, but the man is gone.
That's okay.
I wasn't really talking to him anyway.
This too, I think,
is a type of ghosting.

7.
```
    The ghosts                walk back
        and forth            in my room,
        leaving an X          on the rug
            that won't       vacuum away.
                When I       can't sleep
                    I sit    in the
                      middle
                    of the   cross
                      and    wait.
                But they     don't talk,
            so much as       extend,
        settle               inside me.
```

8.
Grandfather comes as a dozen
            hissing
                        roaches—
the oval shape
        of rebirth
                    suits him,
but
            I still don't
                    understand him.
My father's mother
            is too tired
from the strain
                    of dying
to speak, but

24

I recognize
        the sweet migraine
    of her perfume:
a department store
          mélange of artificial jasmines
my father now keeps
        in a cardboard box
                in his bedroom closet
as out of reach
        as his gun.

9.
Granny
    endures,
      her spirit
             in everything
from
    my mother
to
    every pack of cigarettes
        I'll ever
              smoke—
and in a way,
I'm
    glad
        I was the one
            who lost
her ring.
I know
    she forgives me.
The dead
have more important
    pardons
        to make,
            so
I
    listen.

I am
       always
              listening.
Perhaps that's
      what I miss the most—
I tell
    the bartender
        who has finally
asked me to leave.

            The forgiving.

10.
Not even
my body
can falter
mid-trip
without bruising
remarkably, unforgivingly.
I've been
falling
a lot
lately,
I say
on my way
out.
Into what?
the bartender
asks,
picking me
up.
Myself,
maybe.

11.
I'm learning
      forgiveness,
or at least
              tolerance,
picking
     and peeling
            at my own
                    edges.
My sleep

     is often

  interrupted

by the memory

     of the dry
sound
        of my footsteps
  on a hardwood floor
        in a house now condemned

        where Death
introduced
   itself
           to me,
once
    as a little black cat,
once
       as an overdose,

one grandmother dead,
            the other
                    damned.

12.
The morning after

I realized
        I could never
see
or call
or hug
            her again,

someone wrapped
      the blanket
           she died in
    around me.

If anything,

I'm
    still that child

looping
    her fingers
        through the eyes
           of the crocheted yarn,
pulling it tightly
    around her,
        charmed
by the   absolute
      mystery of life
and the benign ways
          Death touches us.

The way
    the bartender's body
and mine
    wrap around
        each other,

a reunion
        with memories
                of other people

that aren't
     here,

        not anymore,

not
     like this,

in a long
     red booth

 that smells
          a little like
                    her,

     the way
          the squeak

of the pleather
     beneath us

sounds like,

                        listen.

GHOSTS OF LOVE[2]

---

[2] I take lovers like breath,
hold them how my youth
wanted to be held.

Despite enthusiasm,
we are strangers
watching bad television,

exchanging hints of ourselves
until one day
one of us is not here.

I want a love
that needs nothing to exist,
just is.

My ancestors are singing their stories in my ear,
inhabiting my dreams.
I think the moral is I could

lose it all—
the company of a stranger's texts,
half-bitten cigarette butts on my patio.

Sometimes I try
to explain to the lovers
how I am haunted.

Like your house is haunted?
they ask.   *No,* I tell them,
like my body is a site of grief.

BRICKS

In the morning, the bricks were all gone. I yawned into the blinding light of ash-country grey, winter cutting into my mouth like concrete. I accepted the pins in my feet and another day in the place I knew you would not come.

I rented the room from the woman who warned me, *the place has no feng shui*. Unable to resist an east-facing door, I gave her all the money I had, sat on the tub, and wondered, who would put a bath in the middle of such a thing as a bedroom?

When the day grew feet, I put on your jacket. Worn and defiant as you at the neck, I wandered through the art galleries in downtown Santa Fe, trying to hash out the concept of time under the constraint of grief. I wondered if you missed the smell of coffee that accompanied my waking, even when it was a little burnt.

You were not coming back, I told myself over and over, chiseling away at the violence of my new reality with the repetitive abandonment of prayer.

At the cervecería, I pet a cat clawing at a wool rug like the one you had when you lived where you lived when I lived there too.

I thought of your button-up shirts, stain after stain, and the foaming of fabric between my fingers as I massaged lavender castile soap into the threat of permanence. And you, gone now, like the bricks you'd once shown me that had scattered away like our love, in the place I knew you would not come.

HOOK AND LIGHT

I smelled smoke
in your photography studio,
clutched a bag of frozen fish
caught by my brother when I was still married.
I'd had my fill,
which is to say, I'd had none.

Composition says: now glass migrating:
bottle to glass to lips
I drank the tequila I'd brought you as payment—
the welcoming of something new,
the flash, the click
like a heartbeat sick with love.

In front of the camera I tried
to convince myself
I wouldn't just disappear
the memories of home, another self
lifelike.

My journal entry before
asking for the divorce
read simply:
you have something you want to give him,
but you have nothing he wants.

I asked you to take my headshots before deciding
a still life was what I needed
to capture the brevity of a moment.

Yet in the studio,
I fought staging the end of my world—
pan dulce, flowers,
a setting of champagne arranged just so.

I stood frozen,
holding the cold brick of fish.

You reached out,
steadied my trembling
until you were a vein pumping blood back
into my body
like a fish going upstream.

When I want to speak the most is when
I'm out of breath.
After we got dressed,
I mumbled about wanting to disappear
a vow, a shattering—

I thought as my lover
you should have asked about the fish.
*Sorrow can be dangerous when the body
is on fire with empty,*
I tried to explain.
You said nothing.

The way the lights illuminated absence and
presence, I looked at you and saw
hook and light.
Still frozen, you said,
your naked toe nudging the icy walleye
then *test flash,*
before snapping a picture of me

my absence and presence
briefly blinded, I smelled smoke,
didn't disappear—
not even for a moment,
not even on the inside.

We sat quietly chewing pan dulce,
waiting for the fish to thaw.

I THINK I MIGHT BE THE TOXIC PERSON YOU NEED TO CUT OUT OF YOUR LIFE

There are exits inside me
built of foraged material:
loquat branches and pallets
stained with cats' breath,
sticks pulled from mouths
canine and mine,
a set of mystery keys,
every lighter I've ever stolen—
anything they can find.

Let me try to explain the flavor
of not having you:
living off salt
and coffee grounds,
coins licked from the pavement
outside drive-thru windows,
drunk again—

how thirsty it makes me
for your ordinary fingers.

Night beckons street noise.
An entrance becomes an exit.

I still sleep in
the shape of your negative space.
I taught myself things I can't unlearn:
sucking my lips and bumming cigarettes.
I don't really want to quit,
but everyone tells me I should.

Street noise beckons night.
An exit becomes an entrance.
I adored you, and then—
nothing.

Let me try and thank you for hiding
all of the knives
and this feeling of faking it,
though whatever it is I've clawed open—
we won't survive.

BEAUTIFUL, BEAUTIFUL

Bathed in insomnia our bodies begged to open
from fists into palms of night—
you and I became erect lines of flame in the dark,
made love comforted by clutter, lost track of a leg,
a hand, a mouth
in between gasps fueled by indelicate delicacies
that lock of hair that always fell
into my open mouth.
What I'll miss most—
undisguised midnights,
whispering *beautiful, beautiful,* with the resonance of
a psalm,
the precision of your tongue against my neck
as you chanted a name I finally recognized
as my own.

SPIT

I can't remember the first time I watched him peel an orange, but now I can't see one without thinking of him. His thumb bent sharply, nails slicing into the skin, lifting the white pith away from the pulp. He ate citrus for breakfast, lunch, dessert, and with a glass of liquor whenever he craved indulgence. After sex, he'd leave the bed and return with a snifter of mezcal and a wedge of mandarin dripping juice between his teeth. He'd bite it in half, slurping the wound loudly, then offer me the other piece. He held it just out of reach, forcing me to slip out of the sheets, my fingers stretching to accept his bait. I'd pop it into my mouth and watch him watch me, wondering if this was intimacy. He was always watching, always finding a stray hair to brush from my face or a drop of juice to lick away from my chin. Sometimes when he reached for me, I'd close my eyes and let the brightness of his scent wash over me like music. Like birth.

Tonight, the coyotes circle the city, howling after ambulances, and the old flavor of his name lingers on my lips. I try not to feed on memory, but what I've summoned isn't like food. It's more like air, saturating every breath. I press my thumbnail into the pole of a navel orange, making a small circle I peel away, like a puzzle I'm dismantling. But there's no box to slip the thought of him into, only the microzest unzipping into the air, surrounding me with a sudden, jolting presence. It's like he's here, his breath looming in my hand. I rip the entire peel from the flesh, the pith tearing softly in my grip. Something about the softness breaks me. Slice by slice, I make the thought of him disappear into my mouth. I know I'll dream of him tonight.

The first time I made him a drink, I held it out and just as he reached for it, I pulled it back and spit into it. I told him it was a love spell, whispered by the ghosts that haunted me. The second I said it, I knew it was true. Our eyes locked, and I waited for him to match my boldness. He looked at me in that way he would only ever look at me from then on—boldly. He grabbed the bourbon, bitters, orange peel, and spit, and in one long gulp, cursed us both. Then he began to cough. Slowly at first, but soon his little gasps turned desperate.

At first, I thought he had choked on the alcohol or the thought of drinking my spit, but then I knew: he was choking on the magic. His eyes turned red, his hands white. He pounded his chest. His struggle—a mirror to my love—waiting for someone to pull something out. I froze, waiting to see if he'd breathe again. Finally, he reached down his throat and pulled the narrow peel of orange free.

Tell me about your ghosts, he said, the pink returning to his lips as they peeled into a smile, *and I'll show you mine*. I didn't realize until after he was gone that this was the curse—not that he had ghosts to show me, but that eventually, he would become one of mine.

For years I let him peel back my skin, taste the pulp, crack open one bitter seed after another. I poured sadness into him like the glass would never fill up. To say we were close was to miss the point entirely. I watched him choke on me, and I did nothing.

TRAPPED

Despite my sorrows,
I am no lady
still,
he kneels at my feet
like a boy.

I love his promises—
they shine in his mouth
like coins
before betrayal.

He tells me
my pretty face is a trap.
Come here,
it says,
pulling him in
like rain-swollen branches.

Does he see it?
The way my mouth prays
without language.
Porfa.
You're already mine.

Come here,
he tries to command
but it drips
with the plea
of a novena.

The ghosts know
where my love is buried:
past forgiveness,
beneath a name
I no longer answer to.

There's no room left
on my altar
for another martyr.
I light
the last candle
for a sinner
I might've kept.

ANGEL

This body remembers
the small angel of sleep,
before the bloom
of a scream so loud
I knew at once
it was mine.
I still hear it—
dripping into
the stunned emptiness
of night:
drops of blood
on seal-skin tile.
This body.
This ache.
Hotel room withdrawal.
Paper cup chamomile.
His apology,
wringing in my hands.
Bracing for the impact
that comes
in sleep's brute stead.
His voice,
exhaling a plea
to forgive.
But like rest,
this modest halo
cannot envelop
one more broken thing.
I try
to take my hands apart,
to have it mean
what I need to say.

Once,
I fell to the floor
pouring red.

This body.
The feeling.
This is what
I'm left with.

LAMB

Home alone, the television stays on
keeps me company during quiet tasks—
when everything feels like birth.
Maybe I'm paranoid
maybe I could leave
the locks undone, let them click open
without incident
no, that is incidental
says the charming cannibal on screen.
It's always the same stories:
cold case horrors
programs programming me
to remember how easy it is to die
from love.

I used to tell you, it wasn't natural
what we had—
I know it when I see it
hear it, taste the bitter of it
the way we fought
a loud habit I couldn't break
but *I* could break
I knew it well
felt the shards of myself in my hands.

Your voice was a vicious dial tone
a command I couldn't ignore:
your finger lingered
on my arm too long
you wanted to peel my face away
what is its nature?
I finish folding the towels.

I left a note on the table:
gone.
I disappeared
in ways,

so did you.
Still,
I wait for the devil
to balance the scales
to spit in my drink.

The doors can't lock tight enough
to keep out the idea of you.
I've learned which closets are best for hiding—
slip into corners, practice
how to quiet my breath into nothing.

Maybe they're right—
maybe I am paranoid

after all was said and done
I was
a girl
pulling at her own face
just to make sure
it was still there.

ARE YOU OKAY?

Are you okay?
my friend asks. *You
are writing sad poems again—*
I disconnect
the call but

the points
line up like knots of growth
in the tomatillo boughs,
blooms fat off of sunblaze
and sugar water,
craving ritual traffic though rooted
in place. I watch their green paper
veils tremble at the sight of a bee—
it's biology: to survive,
they need a companion
to share an unkempt sting
and my eyes are
two hungry fledglings that watch
you unfurl and scatter
the seeds of what you did to make me
no longer love the way I once could
without even trying,
the body is a root that reaches down
into whatever surrounds it—
like my knees pressing down
into the dirt, half-hoping
that something will blossom,
anchor me here,
but when our lips meet it stings,
our love nothing
more than a whimper now—
gone.

DEFORMING

I wrote down the ways you said you loved me
on the leaves of a Sansevieria—

watched them stretch, grow—
every snake tongue scarred wry with its own
scant love rising, cruelly pale.

On your birthday I stopped watering the plant,
let the leaves dry up on my cold windowsill,
burned them when I no longer feared forgetting.

Put the embers in an envelope,
buried it

the way you deform a thing:
love it
and then don't.

PHILADELPHIA

You said you knew you were in love with me
the night I broke your dead father's last crystal
glass
and you didn't use the biggest shard to slit my
throat.

Let me examine once more
the treasury of moments
leading up to this particular one.

Is it possible it didn't all unravel
like the city across the water
like oxblood braided leather across my cheek?

The best-loved lies are the ones we still believe
I tell you about a pair of stamps the local barfly
carries
from his dead grandmother's collection:

Independence Hall, ten cents apiece
He thinks one day they'll be worth more than
this memory he's carried for years—

something even more precious than
your dead father's crystal.
The moment you told me you'd never been to
Philadelphia

I knew it was over—
you'd missed what was right
in front of you
and for so long,

so had I.

SECOND THOUGHTS

I don't trust the way
my body
falls to the floor
poisoned by missing you.

DESPITE THE DANGER

You pour yourself slowly into me,
careful not to drown out my pain with yours.
It's important to honor the unique wreckage
we've each endured—
how it sits in our bones like silence,
how it's come to feel like home.

I tell you, *move closer*,
ask you to name the softest parts of me,
ask you to give like nothing was ever taken.

I listen to your stories about the love that went sour
how you still fed on it because it was the only thing to eat.

I watch you kiss each one of my scars
until I forget the shape of the hands that gifted them to me.

There is commonality in having endured
the perfect illusion of love.
There is passion in refusing to look away
from what we're afraid of,
from what we've named Ugly.

We choose not to care about the certainty of loss
and instead revel in the ecstasy of this moment—
you let me hold you,
welcome my lips, despite the danger.

We rename each uncertainty
a different word for love,
count each laugh that falls out of us as we bring
down the ceiling plaster
with every thrust of the headboard into the wall.

If you and I are destined to become a poem,
this is where I slow down, like a scorpion hunting
a shadow,

this is where I breathe
like I am being fucked.

This is where the language I use
becomes
my tongue:
sticking out in the direction of home.

HOW IS OUR LOVE RELATED TO YOUR TRAUMA, HE ASKS

How is our love related to your trauma, he asks
as I climb onto the rim of the bathtub.
The floor is the color of dried blood,
no one picked it—it just was,
glossy as my legs collecting
tangled hues of veiny bruises.
Running into things on purpose, he says.
I explain how my body blooms inherited spots
of sorrow,
the soft kicks of the dead that show me where
it hurts—
solvent commands whispered in my ear.

How my thumbs will roll a cigarette without my
telling them to,
cigarettes made of sugar packets and straw paper.
It's bad for the environment, I tell them.
How my legs swing out from bed in the morning
on their own,
run outside and walk up the tree in the yard,
mimic fruit-rot falling in the slightest gale.

This is the last straw,
he tells me through the bathroom door,
sharp as a point he's trying to prove—
a point he's honing into an arrow.
All he needs now is a feather and taut cord
and he will have his weapon.
My feet grip the tub because the floor is lava.

I practice the ritual of alarm,
signal conspecifics to the danger.
It's difficult to localize
or explain self-sacrifice.

Vandalism, he calls it.
It's all so simple—
how the frail bough of love,
wild and weighted with unopened blossoms
breaks from the dueling forces of rot
and bloom
climbing and choking,
both predator
and prey.

FLAT

We drove eight hours through the desert,
heated milkshakes and car silence,
you eating chips out of my dirty hand,
sand sparkle wedged under fingernails and gums.

One of us was half-drunk and muttering,
flat flat flatflatflat, through glittering teeth.

Everything was shimmer and rock,
rotgut earth and tequila.

We saw ourselves in the flies
walking on our gas station skins,
nodded sand out of our ears like stray dogs,
opened our mouths, felt our insides dry up.

We kept saying, *you could die out here.*

I thought about the migrants,
their missing children, and tried not to fall apart.

The crisp closeness of us as we passed
the bottle was such a delicate thing—
I knew what it meant to fall into a hole
and call it shelter,
that all mass graves have always been
man-made.

That night the dusken landscape
was so tenderly certain,
we could hear it sing.

In the dark you fumbled for the hotel light.
I remember
how the dimness coiled around and around us
like regret.

How I tried to remember what it was we'd
forgotten to do,
how it was so very *very* much.

How I watched you peel the plastic
wrap from a sanitized tumbler,
drink glass after glass
from the bathroom sink
then slam it, empty, on the counter,
never offering it to me.

How you breathed out my wanting,
how I could only inhale it.
How I felt my insides
dry up.

HOLD ME, DAMN IT

Without realizing
I hear myself saying
hold me, damn it—
or it could have been
you
or the television
I suppose
even the neighbors—
it makes sense
doesn't it?
When it comes down to it,
we all just want
to be held.

ETYMOLOGY

His name doesn't mean forest or tree or God
but a sound, like

whoosh.

Like air blown over a beer
you just can't finish at the bar.

One too many failed relationships
have proven the theory
that the Sun will go out—

but for now,

his name in my throat
just to prove a point.

I've heard love is related to time,

a well-oiled pocket knife
we open and close

again
and again—

not a weapon, exactly

but not *not* a weapon.

CHEERS

To the small stuff,
to the snippets of conversations
and cocktails that make you lick your lips and say,
oh, that's good.

To you,
to the evidence of us
to the animal hunger
that told us how.

To embracing the primordial importance of joy,
like my fingers around this glass,
or your name dissolving under my salted tongue
sucking
your curls in the great emptiness of my mouth.

To weaning ourselves from sadness
by leaning into these,
the smallest things,
where love is always hiding.

BACKDRAFT

I am between a thing:
the space between go and gone—

I thought you would be here, too,
barefoot in my kitchen
looking for something to eat,
watering the houseplant in the corner
that I always seem to forget.

Instead I am looking for you
in the pages of books you never read,
in rough drafts and whiskey,
in the empty spots where your things were
in our so-called home.

I confront my complicity in our love's demise:
I wanted to believe the lie,
let you think it, too.
I poured kerosene onto a wildfire
then said, *I love you, goodnight.*

I dreamt we were driving in your car—
I begged you to turn left
but instead, you turned right.
When I awoke,
I knew it was over between us.

Let me be this grief,
this remnant of love.
Let me be anything else but that person, that
night, with that version of you.
Let me forget this place
where my body was reduced to a heap of ash,
aching,
reaching for the hand that had snuffed it out like
an unwanted cigarette.

Let me be the warning that should you ever try to
hold me again,
I will cauterize the desire that ails you.

No, my blood did not put out the flames,
no, I did not stop loving you before the backdraft
blew us apart—

on fire,
out of time.

This is not how
I wanted us to die.

TO LOVE IS TO CHANGE EVERYTHING

There you are
and here I am,
not quite awake,
or asleep,
still—

it feels like home between ourselves.
I want to tell you everything
and nothing at the same time:
please don't mind my
desperation to know you.

Paradise is fragile by nature,
was created to be taken away,

but I'm not a thief—
I'm a lover
circumnavigating hope
like a gallery of antique
chairs not to be sat upon.

You and I break
furniture when we touch,
and when the legs
give way from under us—
I feel more like myself
than ever before.

GHOSTS OF SELF[3]

---

[3] Right in the center of me
is a hole that cannot be filled   even by the
biggest hands
or the recent years   or a lifetime supply of
Turkish cigarettes.

The body can tolerate all kinds of love—
can forget
until the need comes to a head

until it's been years since you left
since I gave a damn
about love   or quitting smokes
or the tying together of years   or my tongue
spitting out the words
I'll never love again,

until the feeling becomes conviction
becomes   who I am   becomes even bigger
than my body
fills the smoky rooms
I'm always running in and out of
trying to find the you that will love
me,
that will tolerate love

and I don't mind
because the body can tolerate
all kinds of empty
until it's nothing
but a pair of hands
gloved in age spots
taking a cigarette out of the box
then sliding it back in.

DEFINING LOSS

1 a: suddenly a word
// a buzz under my tongue
    b: a word I could have sworn meant as much
      as I do
// even when I don't feel like much

2 a: a severing motion
     an opening and a closing
// well wishes for a death
    I'll confront again and again
// wailing room to room
    b: a wound some other deemed necessary
// the way winds reverse oceans
    the way I panic when I realize the swindle
    c: why this word
// why this wound
    d: why this you
// why this trainwreck of a place

3 a: my life unsettled
// chewing on the yellow edges of leaves
    until I see something godlike
    b: uncanny at this lemon hour
// to live another day sleep can claim
    c: well-rested for death

4 a: if only my body was not to knowledge
    as a drop is to the ocean
    so when my tongue-tethered heart leapt out
    from me
// it might buoy us through the riptide of life
    pouring from the sky
    b: telling us to forget our injuries
// I feel I am close
// like a word someone taught me
    c: but now I've lost

5 a: my hair, thick as a school of gaping fish,
     could drown a man and his
     sorrow
// and my limbs, I feel, are vanishing underwater,
     I am becoming an island
     my head falls back and anchors my
     torpedo-like torso, buoyant with this
     pulse ticking
    b: how are they going to tell me a damn thing
// when they don't know if I'm a womb or
    c: a bomb

CARDINAL

That summer the grass just kept coming
full of life and color and your words
poking into my memory
the futility of them
like the blades under my feet
a type of inescapability

you wouldn't touch me
didn't want the blood of your dead child
to mark you, though we both knew
there was no
fooling god.

I lost count of the cardinals that came to me
unlike the mercy I so desperately needed
drops of red in the yard you never called ours
gathering material for their nests
I didn't—*couldn't*—unknow the shame of naming
a question with an answer
(not so much named but wanted
which is in a way, to name)
the way the cardinals did
with direction.

Everything began to feel *urgent*
the room spinning
the blood touching everything
that touched me
even when the bleeding stopped
you wouldn't touch me
so today
when I found myself mowing the grass
straight down
to its sudden roots
flitting back and forth across the front yard
a hundred and two fahrenheit
the thinness of it

pushing the heavy burden
of the mower away from me
yet grasping it to myself
I knew to name the feeling
grief.

I ran until my father pulled up in his truck
looking at me, without really looking at me
(by chance, the way you did)
there to pick up the tool he'd lent me again
to make it clear
I was his divorced daughter
with an overgrown lawn
no husband to mow it
no baby to speak of
so of course he demanded I *at least*
mow my lawn.

I wanted to grab my father
by his proud shrinking shoulders
to show him
the bouquets of condolences
wilting on the kitchen counter

See the instinctively naive Alstroemeria?
The sexless wax of the ornamental fern?

To tell him
how I miscarried what I wanted
more than anything
how the birds were everywhere now
those stupid fucking cardinals
a sign they say
but for whom?
For me: how alone one could suddenly feel
in their body.

I wanted to point to the dead
and sunken places upon me
hoping somehow my grief
would be recognized

instead
quiet
as in, *my grief didn't make a sound.*
I didn't know what tool to ask for.
I stood alone in my body
watched the lopped grass wilt in the heat,
wondered if nothing else
could I be buried in this
the stillness of a field after the stirring.
I braced for the impact of going limp but only
locked eyes with the woman across the street
a matriarch whistling after her unleashed dog
a little copper thing bounding across the street
after the cardinals returning to my yard.

1: of basic importance
as in, *a cardinal principle*
2: very serious or grave
as in, *a cardinal sin*
I admit, like the dog
I was worn out from the chase.

When the rain stopped
the roots of grass dried like knots of eyes closing
a portrait of my barren summer—
still the sky reached for me with its cardinals.

One by one
my limbs fell asleep
waiting for you to touch them
the garden lay in ruins wailing of cicadas
waiting to be guided into wet

and ready earth
their rhythm not unlike the ultrasounding of a tiny
heartbeat.

Still, I slept in agony
tried to gather the pieces of myself I'd left
when I thought you were home.
I didn't want a metaphor.

I didn't even want you back.
I wanted the child you never called ours
my little death unborn
and I wanted someone else, anyone
to say their name.

GEOMETRY OF HUNGER
(For Tiffany)

Sepia portrait of the day spent
boiling apples in vinegar:
resistance—how crimson skins pucker yet remain.

After centuries of poaching, elephants that no
longer grow tusks,
he doesn't like to eat inside because *the smell
attracts feral cats.*

So we've come to the beach
where the light is green
when the hungry earth chips away
at our empty china,

tectonic plates driven by the shape of the moon,
we sit watching a tree that the ocean doesn't know
if it wants to keep or spit out.

I count circles within circles,
cork between my lips,
in the distance workers cut down
an invasive breed—

they will keep the good wood, but how
do they know
which are the good parts of a femme like me?

Will they keep a damn thing?
Bother
to bleach, bisect bone, count the rings,
notice the bruises, the growth?

I'm hungry for a door that won't fail
to catch the lock
when terror falls like fangs.

More than anything—to resist that dream
altogether
and enjoy a pickled apple on the beach with you.

IT TURNS OUT THAT NO ONE THINKS I'M A BIRD

I move pebbles with my mouth hoping to trick the birds into thinking I'm one of them. When I sleep, they take all of my shoes and string them from telephone lines in an obscene gesture. It's so difficult trying to make friends these days.

I RESEARCH MAD WOMEN

I.
Salome smokes two packs a day
cracks crawfish heads
slurps down vitamins
waltzes to the rattle of bees
sew-sew lobotomy
seven veils
king
acrobat thighs toss
turntable albatross
pick the right song at the party dear
she can dance on her hands
daughter of air.

II.
Who's afraid of Virginia Woolf?
those of silence
or a book
be they Anon or a mouse
the poof was rocks in her blouse
sometimes a man or a sea-bound child
with rats of hair uncombed and wild
skeletons fall and it's indecent
and human nature all too recent
as is her pet, a marmoset
possessed by devils
she once had met.

III.
Sylvia calls everyone Daddy
no one knows what to think about it
the prison is us, she tells me, *thus*
a coffin is a coffin
and some do raise the lid
a lady is a Lazarus
and some do raise the dead.

GOSSIP

*The fact that the Sun hasn't burned us all up
is a mystery,* I hear the tomatoes whispering,
soft and split and shining,
infecting another dream at the dead end
of another late morning that's
already too hot not to be called afternoon.

*The woman who lives here—
why doesn't she water us?
Why does she just stand there looking out the window?
Watching the heat pinch our faces,
never leaving her house—
as if she's afraid of us,
no longer trusts something she has to nurture.*

It's just that I'm allergic to bees, I say to no one
knowing damn well it's a lie.

YOUTH

You   pluck

         the burs

                from   my   throat

try   to teach me
              how to speak   in
verse.

Maybe   you   know

        all the rules
   that   need
         breaking

    it is   more likely
               that
                  you do not,
still,
    I let myself   fall

              down the path—
(if you   can call
             something that goes
     nowhere
           a path)
toward
     what is now only
             obligation,
my tongue
      tugging   out

  the broken glass
                      in the
dirt

       so I might

              open   the sutures

        you   thought
           you could

                make me forget,

     blood

          percolating

               through the cracks.

The burden

    of my biology:

        to mother

     flesh split

           by my own   bite,

to heal,

    harden,

        mark

   clue

     to cue

        caution

why

   am I made

           of such   fragile

                 things?

EMBERS

I was trying to identify the species that raised my bones like sticks for a fire, a beacon of the muteness of a hurt I still don't understand but feel nonetheless, and while I sat burning I thought about what I had done to deserve this and was surprised to find that it wasn't nothing.

CRACKED MIRROR

We're taught what a house is
never what it can do
I wish I were like that, steady
my awe shivering through static
like walking backward—
looking for cracks in an emptiness
I once called home
borrow a body, ask for its endlessness
pour everything into it
like a reverse birth:
wading into water
touching memory once more
was it a bad dream or a haunting?
To not know is not failure.
If everyone you love is going to die
what do you think will happen to you?
Will you continue
or start again?

                                      Do you continue,
                                         or start again?
                               What happens to you
                     when everyone you love is dead?
                        To not know is not failure.
               Was it a bad dream or a haunting?
                          Memory of water
                              birth in reverse
   pouring everything into a borrowed body
                               empty, endless
                       like walking backward—
searching for cracks in what you called home
               my awe shivers through static
                   I wish I were like that, steady.
                  We're taught what a house is
                        not what it can hold.

PENUMBRA

Horoscope said
someone is trying to get close to you.

The guests had gone home,
the leftovers spooned into a red-lidded dish,
and the version of you I knew
had left me
pining in the kitchen.

Blues on our neighbor's pawnshop radio
they all went to heaven in a little row boat
I clapped my hands and said nothing
I went outside,
looked at the moon
where I would sometimes hide.

I never knew what to say when you were
around—
a good listener,
a keeper of precious details.
I didn't want to be perceived;
I wanted to be loved.
I wanted proof
and I wanted to leave none.

Horoscope said
*to get close, you must surrender your weapons
as if for the first time.*

I already knew anything could be a weapon
in the wrong hands—
especially love.

Everytime I wanted to say *I love you*, and didn't
I felt like I was stealing from you.
Wondered, *is that a weapon?*

I came inside and pretended I was brave,
opened the wound of my mouth and told you:

There's an eclipse.
Oh yeah? You asked. *What's it look like?*
Dusty. I mumbled. *Like film.*
What?
My voice was a sliver, thinner than shadow.
It's fading, I said. *But still there.*

What I wanted was to crawl into your skin.
What I mean is I wanted to feel close to you,
but I could only mumble one thing
and then repeat
another, entirely different thing—
a jazz refrain.

Horoscope said
practice unfulfilled desire—
endure desire for the sake of desire.

Was it sort of low on the horizon? You asked.
Yes, low and glowing.
Hmm? You hadn't heard me.
Yes, I said. *Low and pulsing ripe with light.*

I should've stopped there,
but wanted the impossible—
to say something that could exist as truth
between us,
as if truth were a bridge,
a crossing of two lovers
framed in moonlight.

Its penumbra was so vivid, I said.
It felt close.

Close? you echoed, asking me for a word I was
certain of until your asking made me doubt it.

What did I know?
What did I *think* I knew?

Horoscope said
you know what closeness is,
and what it is not.

Silence bloomed, as it always did
under my heavy tongue.
You peeled open the window,
let the sickly-sweet grape blossoms of mountain
laurel climb in and settle between us.

Horoscope said
there's a time and a place for lightness
it's just not now
or here.

Why did words slip away from me?
I had talked to the moon since I was a child.
I knew the curves of her face, even in darkness
especially then.

Stupid tender tongue,
stupid thinking I'd been stealing from you,
when the whole time I'd been picking
my own pockets.

I followed you into the bedroom,
pondered the experience of your body
as it eclipsed our white cotton sheets,
made note of the way silence forged into your skin
like a scar, like a kiss—
was it really only shadow?

What I want to tell you:
when I'm surrounded in darkness,
what I see is not the moon so much as
the light that casts from you—
always as if for the first time.

Horoscope said
you are the room you're standing in.

EMPTINESS

Like a holiday
you can't turn it off

like a bone
you can't take it out

you rationalize you should be able to
and still you can't.

Think about it too long and you will
bear a son in its name
stop thinking and you might die

become a door to the door
of emptiness within you.

The big prize—
the rescue you crave—
the momentum of theatrics
makes it too sentimental to throw away

so you let it linger
endure it
learn to depend upon it
whistle to it
kneel even
devotional

because the truth is you've evolved.
The truth is you no longer think on your feet
but on your hands and knees
your heart parallel to your personal demons
training for the execution,
looking at the faults in the floor.
You can't help but notice the shapes you made
there, when you were trying to land somewhere
different.

WHAT STAYED IN MY SKIN

The moment I realize each name I've been given
is one instruction after another for building a cage—
is the moment I deliver myself from the exhaustion
of erecting my bones like cards
for anything but escape.

I say my name backward,
rub salt into my shoulders.
These days I'm neither cave nor whetstone—
not a thing easily haunted
save what's stayed in my skin,
half-wishing they'd killed me
if only for a second,
if only to vanquish the sorrow they'd birthed
like a bear sniffs a dead thing
then fades warless into trees.

The sober weightlessness of it, merry as dawn—
I eat all the plants shaped like tongues,
oversleep in shadows I shape with twigs,
shed fur and skin, sun-bleach tattoos,
beat demons from my heart with tin spoons,
spit out wisdom teeth like grapefruit seeds.
Soon I will have rid myself of enough of me not to be
a christened vessel darned with freshly cut laurel,
toeing the line of my chances.

I learned the magic communing with ghosts—
a vocabulary with eyes closed,
the lesson of ripping myself awake,
of listening to stray dogs bark,
of watching dust copulate and knowing that soon
it will be me.

There are as many exits as people, I've been told,
the salty anchor of our encounters turns the sea a
bitter green

I wade knee-deep into year after year,
open my mouth and let name after name spill
down my throat.

The idle imbalance of chemicals in my
baseball cap overcrowds my organs with
genetically modified dreams
waking delicately into what feels real—I see
stallions pawing mounds of salt into the path
cut differently now, martyred.
I scribble name after name in the sand—
what we've learned from our pain,
what we're still learning I braid into my hair,
let it grow, echo.
When it stills, I pause,
listen for what resonates before continuing—
I know death is not an escape,
it is only a door
slamming open and shut.
Sometimes
it is the form that fills the frame
we recognize as ourselves
in a look or a gesture,
wishing more than anything
we did not.

AWAKENING

I have stared into mirrors as if they held keys
just beyond the glass,
keys to a good night's sleep, keys to open
a trunk of vanishing ghosts I've loved
and the love we finally unlatched
from our brass buckled egos.

After studying the moon
one writer concluded:
it's never too late to have a happy childhood.
I've been both entrance and exit
for the living and dead
and have found that it's never too late
to feel at home in your body.

I've been told where the keys are kept
I've been shown where the mirrors lay,
but I always wake up—
my finger curling back from a point of direction
into one indefinite gesture before infinite others
curling into myself
listing what's reflected in my lover's eyes:
window, door, person piecing themself
back together, an ugly or noble task
depending on the angle.

Where'd you go?
I hear a distant memory ask
I'm looking at the moon.
Does that make me a slut?

My lover rolls out our new knives
from their linen skin,
shows me how to slice scallions
paper-thin by rocking the blade for-
ward, one little circle
after another.

It feels dangerous—
I'm scared to cut off a finger.
Love feels so much bigger than a finger,
less dexterous, too.
Pinch it back.
Like this.

I admit defeat
opt to peel the carrots instead.
I'm learning to protect my magic
from black holes and love that cuts.

The thing about those moonlit nights
is we had 'em all
until we didn't.

Ravaged by love,
I was a ruin crumbling at the joist—
ravaged by time equals distance from you,
I was design emerging from the debris.

The ache of it dulls and swells,
punctuates how ready I am—
or not.

CODA FOR ANDROMEDA

1.
For
giving my
        mother (self),
like anything,
      is tethered
           to the construct of time:
there is the rock of it,
the chain,
always—
a letting go.
    I'm no longer
        practicing
            my addiction—
mapping routes
      to loneliness
           (there is no opportunity for love
                I have not missed).
In this story:
I'm small,
      all she has
      a wonderful, terrifying thing.
We race to the front door,
drive all night.
        My entire world
is watching her
coastal-green eyes
reflected in the rearview mirror,
wondering when she will
look at me. Love can feel
like waiting. Like erasure.
But in the story
I'll tell you,
      the love
         is generous,
              unwounded.

(*Hello,*   little kicks)
       are you listening?

2.
Still, the memory—
       better to be offered
       than abandoned
my sister, afraid,
              because I didn't want to be alone.
There are scars you'll point to
              and ask:
                     What happened here?
Now the trick:
       to unwound what survived me.
To open a door—
       (it's a body, not a door)
To mother—
       to gather, to unify,
              to become a place of convergence
                     (my edges lignify
                            with irrevocable want).
I've kept every key—
       but for what hope?
              To come home.
Mirrors lay me bare.
       but this clarity—
              what does it serve?
I dreamt that my father poured air
into a mezcal glass and called it love.
              I drank.
                     Woke,
                            salt carving another flaw into
the lip
of the retreating tide of how I'd imagined my
life.
There are no pictures of us
all together.

       Still—
            we were.

3.
I have so much to give you
beyond myth, sacrifice,
beyond what's meant
       to be set down.
You grow wings
(the monster is not appeased but irrelevant).
I'm learning to be sky,
      not cage—
I want
to love you
beyond the narrow reach
of the small place
      that has been
           my heart.
While I still have this body,
I beg of you:
take from it what you need—
        forgetfulness,
        breath,
        the red in my hair,
        one language after another
        until we understand.
This is where I find you:
      in design,
           pulsating—
not in the body's repetition,
but in surrender.

I'm pregnant.
      We are safe.

The sea has no teeth
      where we're going.

NOTES

"Lamb" includes both lines inspired by and direct quotations from the author's favorite film, *The Silence of the Lambs*.

The narrator's question in "Cardinal," "*could I be buried in this,*" refers to Allison Benis White's poetry collection *Please Bury Me in This*.

The poem "Flat" references the ongoing reality that, as of today, thousands of migrants, many of them children, remain missing in the United States. These disappearances are not accidents; they are the result of a system that treats human lives as disposable—especially those seeking refuge, safety, and dignity. The author wishes to acknowledge that the landscape of this poem is stolen land, in honor of the Indigenous peoples whose ancestral territories we occupy—many of whom also continue to disappear without justice. These disappearances are not isolated tragedies; they are part of a broader and ongoing pattern in which Black, Brown, Indigenous, and migrant bodies are treated as expendable. To write about this is not to claim these stories, but to resist their erasure. May this poem serve as both witness and a small act of remembrance. It is written in solidarity with those still searching, and as a call to witness what continues to be erased.

"Penumbra" incorporates lines adapted from the author's horoscope as written in the Co–Star astrology app.

In "Awakening," the mention of "one author" refers to Tom Robbins and his novel *Still Life with Woodpecker*.

ACKNOWLEDGMENTS

Grateful acknowledgment is made to the following editors of the publications in which these poems, or versions of them, first appeared, sometimes under different titles:

The Acentos Review: "Geometry of Hunger"

Anatolios Magazine: "Going Through That Motion is Surrender" and "When I Leave You Mother, I Don't Bother Saying Goodbye"

Ellipsis... Literature and Art: "Thank You For the Skin"

Great Weather For MEDIA Anthology, Beacon Radiant: "Hook and Light"

Great Weather For MEDIA Anthology, Paper Teller Diorama: "Defining Loss"

Fourteen Hills Magazine: "First You Must Enter"

Orca, A Literary Journal: "Flat"

The Vassar Review: "Sisters"

***

I feel ridiculously lucky to have so many people in my life that have supported my journey, without whom this book wouldn't exist.

To Jennifer Lewis—a true literary force. Your support is sacred. Thank you for giving my writing a home on stage and on the page with Red Light Lit. Your vision and devotion are true gifts, and we're so lucky you share them with us.

To Isra Cheema, for taking time and care with editing these poems—your work made them sharper, braver, better. Thank you for being an immediate friend and inspiration, and for sharing your beautiful imagination with me.

To Sarah Bethe Nelson, for your masterful copyedits and ever-generous curiosity. Your artistic spirit has always been a guide.

To Leah, for capturing so many meaningful moments in my life with such care and vision. You curate beauty with such intention, and this cover is no exception—my heart is full.

To Tanis O'Connor, for encouraging me to push myself as a performer, for reminding me what it means to be a rebel girl, and for all the laughter and space we've shared from here to there. Sometimes you just need to know someone believes in your art and isn't afraid to sit with your darkness. For me, that's been you.

To the city of Austin and to the beautiful weirdos who make it magic. Special thanks also to the City of Austin Economic Development Department for supporting the many art and literary projects I've endeavored in over the years. Thank you for believing in my creative potential.

To San Francisco for always welcoming me back with open arms no matter how much I complain about the cold. I love you.

To my parents Kathy Reyna and Rudy Mendoza. Every day, I hope for more time with you, just to try—however impossibly—to return even a fraction of the love you've poured into me. The ways you've shaped me will stay with me in this life and whatever comes after.

To Tiffany and Ryan Parker, Chris and Tammie Reyna, Allie, Mary, Rosie, Seamus, and Ellie. Thank you for being the kind of family that shows up with love, laughter, and strength. Your support has meant the world to me, and I'm so grateful Andromeda will grow up surrounded by your warmth and wild hearts.

To Sue, who left before I could thank her for being the weirdest person I've ever met and for influencing my creative side in such magical ways. I always felt safe with you. XO, Chartreusie.

To Peter Bullen, Rob Macaisa Colgate, Miah Jeffra, Tomas Moniz, Christine No, Lauren Parker, Linda Ravenswood, and Preeti Vangani. You are literary rockstars in every sense. It has been a joy to share the stage with each of you throughout the years, and it's an unbelievable honor to now hold your words within these pages. Thank you for sitting with these poems and for reminding me what community in art can look like.

To my writing mentors and professors over the years, Jill Gladstein, Geoffrey Green, Andrew Joron, Junse Kim, Michael Krasny, Peter Orner, Caro de Robertis, Peter Schmidt, and Chanan Tigay. Thank you for seeing something in me before I fully saw it myself. Your wisdom, encouragement, and care helped me find the courage to tell my stories. I carry your guidance with deep gratitude into every page I write.

To Kar Johnson. Thank you for every loving book rec, for your unwavering support, and for being the clearest, most consistent example of love I've known since the day we met. You've shown up, again and again, with insight, humor, and a giant heart. You make grief and joy feel more human.

To the many generous, unruly people in my life who have shown up, performed alongside me, fed me, held me, laughed and cried with me. Tandie, Jannah, Shorna, Marshall, Miraç, Diego, Juni, Donovan, Jenny, Daniela, Natassia, Kate, Kelly, Luna, Jenn, Lou, Jori, Albion, Anza, Jeremy, Cristal, Brooke, Blue, SR, Anneleen, Kennedy, Michael, Jonny, Jenny, Niz, Heather, Hannah, Tony, Manni, David, Brad, Danielle, Emily, Gerardo, Aly, Cristin, India, Meredith, May, Kacy, Rich, Steven, Alicia, Kate, Nat, Rebecca, Laura, Christine, Elle, Tiffany, Greer, Chris, Taylor, Dave, Drew, Travis, Rocky, Abraham, David, Juan, Rosemary, Maddie, Felix, Evangeline, Van, Ami, Ari, Carlos, Nate, Jose, Kendra, Christopher, Matt, Austin, Kacy, Jenny, Sofia, Melanie, the Lopez Family, the Fannons, and the Howells. Thank you for all of the kindness, creativity, and joy you've brought into my life.

To my daughter, Andromeda Belle. Thank you for making me a better person, and for showing me, every single day, that there is *always* more love. I love you forever, beyond words, beyond the body, beyond this universe and yours.

And to the ghosts. May you know love in whatever realm you find yourselves in.

ABOUT THE AUTHOR

Loria Mendoza (she/they) is a queer Chicanx author, curator, writing instructor, community art producer, and multidisciplinary artist rooted in Austin, Texas. Drawn to Swarthmore College's commitment to social justice and critical inquiry, Loria graduated with an Honors Major in English Literature and an Honors Minor in Political Science. Their passion for storytelling, equity, and the arts then carried them across the country to San Francisco, where they earned both an MA and MFA in English and Creative Writing at San Francisco State University. There, they discovered a love for community building while serving as a co-curator of the graduate program's Poetry Center reading series, *The Velvet Revolution*, and as Fiction Editor for *14 Hills* magazine.

Their book *Life's Too Short* (Fourteen Hills Press) received the Michael Rubin Book Award. Their work has also been published in the *great weather for MEDIA* anthologies, *Beacon Radiant* and *Paper Teller Diorama, The Vassar Review, Fourteen Hills, ellipsis… literature and art, Orca, A Literary Journal, Moon City Review, Anatolios Magazine, Love Is the Drug & Other Dark Poems: A Poetry Anthology* by *Red Light Lit, Acentos Review, Subprimal, Transfer Magazine*, and more. Their writing has been performed on stages across the United States.

Loria currently lives in Austin with their partner, newborn daughter, two cats named Hall and Oates and a dog named Betty White. They are the curator and host of Red Light Lit Austin and a firm believer in the healing power of art, community, storytelling, and love.

ABOUT RED LIGHT LIT

Red Light Lit is a small press and arts collective producing tightly curated live events that blend poetry, prose, art, dance and music into immersive, interdisciplinary experiences. Each show brings together diverse artists for bold, experimental collaboration, creating performances that deepen connection, build creative community, and leave audiences inspired to make art of their own. With over a decade of momentum, Red Light Lit is a trusted cultural platform for powerful voices and transformative storytelling.

Since its founding in 2013, Red Light Lit has published 10 literary journals; produced more than 300 live shows in cities including Austin, Chicago, Joshua Tree, Los Angeles, Portland, San Francisco and Seattle; and released the poetry anthology *Love Is the Drug & Other Dark Poems* as well as three full-length collections: *Unearth (The Flowers)* by Thea Matthews, *Lions Like Us* by Hollie Hardy, *The Body Can Tolerate* by Loria Mendoza, and Red Light Lit's first novel, *A Road of Her Own*, by Kimberly Gomes is forthcoming in 2026.

PRAISE FOR THE BODY CAN TOLERATE

"Reader, set aside your 'safe word' and enter Loria Mendoza's stunning collection of poems! *The Body Can Tolerate* is a haunting testament to true existence. Where the ghosts are both witnesses and actors; where the grit of living is everywhere articulated. Without equivocation. Without ribbons. Visit this sense of place strewn with a gorgeous, visceral intensity of language. Start from the 'source' material, commonly referred to as family, then move on to the absorbing maze of passions marking adulthood where the promise of freedom through the agency of love dangles dangerously across each page. Or as the poet puts it: 'Let me thank you for hiding / all of the knives.' And hold on reader, because born out of all the marvelously delineated feeling tones of warning in this collection ('this modest halo / cannot envelop / one more broken thing') there is a coda. It's called the future, and the poet shares its spherical music with us."

—**Peter Bullen**, author of *Wallflower*

"'The way you deform a thing: / love it / and then don't.' So too do the poems in Loria Mendoza's debut deform their readers, the balm of language pulling us in until the rawness of experience startles us back out. These poems attend to love but only alongside its loathing, to relationships but only alongside their fracturing, and to great presences as they turn into great absences, ghosts that the speaker lets haunt them so that readers might bear witness. Sweeping across the confessional, the prosaic, and found forms, Mendoza's lyric awes with its directness, its immediacy, and its fearlessness. By this, I do not mean unafraid of pain, but rather unafraid to display that pain in act after act of defiance. The speaker claims: 'The burden / of my biology: / to mother / flesh split / by my own bite.' These poems are exactly that: born from Mendoza's very flesh, split open and mothered for the reader's sake. We are lucky she has decided to do so."

—**Rob Macaisa Colgate**, author of *Hardly Creatures*

"In this boldly intimate collection, identity, memory, and grief swell in a body haunted by history and longing. Body:haunt, corporeal:immaterial. That dialectic and its complications play throughout Mendoza's triptych of ghosts. Traversing dreamscapes, generational trauma, exile, and love's undoing, *The Body Can Tolerate* is a lyrical excavation of survival, something we seek from poetry now more than ever. Here, too, language becomes ritual, and every loss leaves a door swinging open, most often in the dark. Trust Mendoza and walk through it with her."

—**Miah Jeffra**, author of *American Gospel*

"*The Body Can Tolerate* reveals the delicate ways things can haunt us: grandfathers, an orange, body parts, mirrors, desire, childhood. Loria Mendoza crafts a life cycle of poems that will linger long after you read them."

—**Tomas Moniz**, author of *All Friends Are Necessary*

"*The Body Can Tolerate* is a feral, fearless collection that 'burrow[s] like animals, sensing only hunger / to unbury what won't die.' Loria Mendoza examines generational ache and its myriad fruits with brutal, lyric tenderness. These poems hold grief, love and survival to the light until they refract into something holy: a poetics of loss, of an artist's becoming and a woman's emergent wholeness. Generous and necessary, Mendoza draws us a map, builds us a home in which love might be the deepest cut; but it is still the endgame, the ultimate perseverance."

—**Christine No**, author of *Whatever Love Means*

"Mendoza's collection *The Body Can Tolerate* is a lush and heartbreaking mapping of love and grief. Every movement of the collection reads like a breath holding a damning silence. Mendoza writes about loss with a fractal grace and harsh beauty with emotional notes as fierce as a breaking dam."

—**Lauren Parker**, author of *Dark Way Down*

"*'i stood alone in my body'*—loria mendoza's *the body can tolerate* is a subtle but ultimately explosive text.

separated into corridors of exploration, longing, grief, sites of trauma, sites of parental terror, rape, and the ugly, essential therapies of loss and starvation—mendoza parses out paths followed and conversations with shadows along her way.

she stands in thrall of that direct access to a centrality of emotion that an artist-listener can meet. mendoza roars into the vitality she feels—both in and outside her girlbag of blood and bone—in love, aggression, dissociation, through relationships' sweetness and relatedness's brutality.

in one particularly powerful moment, she asserts that her work is made in sites of panic, through landscapes where the body breaks into its ghost song—which, as we know, are oftentimes songs of aching, bristling, familial, historical uncertainty. mendoza's path calls on a kind of personal bravery that most writers are only able to skim. where other artists tickle toward and point to, mendoza leans in, arms reaching, seemingly undaunted by fear of going so far out with little left to return her home.

mendoza journeys in—with a cudgel and a velvet trumpet. she has no map or promise of safety, just a table of contents and a steady circling round overlays of ache and longing. mendoza goes 'there'—not unafraid, but determined to ask, *and then where!? what have you taken us to!?*"

—**Linda Ravenswood**, author of *Cantadora: Letters from California*

"Vivid in its lyricism, Loria Mendoza's *The Body Can Tolerate* is a poetry of acute and tender witnessing, 'to unbury what won't die.' Traversing cunning pavements and crooked bangs, her poems are capacious in their varied forms to hold the unsteady intensities of grief as violence accrues in the speaker's life. A haunting, image-rich collection of familial strife, of threatened girlhood, of the perils of loving, of woman enduring and persisting despite and alongside her myriad ghosts."

—**Preeti Vangani**, author of *Mother Tongue Apologize*

www.ingramcontent.com/pod-product-compliance
Lightning Source LLC
Chambersburg PA
CBHW050330010526
44119CB00050B/733